"I have been involved in personal dev
have been friends with and associated w
in this industry but I have not met anyone who has taken the laws of
success and shared them with others in a more effective manner."

~ Bob Proctor

"I have personally observed Jacquelyn MacKenzie's focus and habits
around making money over the past several years. Her strongest suit is
her ability to teach solid principles to her clients about having the right
mindset and thinking to change their habits to ensure their businesses
thrive. One after another, the entrepreneurs she helps explodes their
businesses. This book is a world class example of how to succeed in
business and in life."

~ Mick Petersen, International Bestselling author
of *Stella and the Timekeepers*

"Simple, elegant and profound. These three words perfectly describe
Jacquelyn's book. Implement these ideas in your life and experience a
glorious transformation."

~ Banafsheh Akhlaghi International Best Selling Author
of *Beautiful Reminders ~ Anew*

"Jacquelyn has an incredible intuition about what businesses need. Her
advice to me and my management team has had incredible impact. Just one
simple exercise changed our profitability by $121,000 in the last ten days of
the same month."

~ Bob Taylor President & CEO Alliant Healthcare Services

"As a Business man I want profit. This book is a must read if you are serious
about major profit increase. Jacquelyn gives you the tools and process you
need to think into result of maximum profit."

~Wayne Kuhn, Broker, Remax Real Estate Centre Inc.

Jacquelyn –

The Prophet of Profit

**Let the PROFIT grow in all
areas of your life starting today!**

Jacquelyn MacKenzie

Published by
Hasmark Publishing, judy@hasmarkservices.com

Permission should be addressed in writing to Jacquelyn here:
info@jacquelynmackenzie.com

Editor, Nita Robinson
www.NitaHelpingHand.com

Cover Design & Layout, Anne Karklins
annekarklins@gmail.com

Photography, Peter Hurley
www.peterhurley.com

ISBN-13: 978-1-988071-40-4
ISBN-10: 1988071402

Dedication

There are so many people in my life that I am grateful for, but first and foremost, I am grateful for my three boys. When I look at your sweet faces, you inspire me to no end, you mean everything to me, and you are the motivating reason I do what I do. I am truly honored that you picked me to be your mom. I dedicate this book to you because it is what I want for you.

To my clients, you continue to blow me away with everything you are doing and going after. You are inspiring people all around you. I am happy and excited for you. I am in awe of you!

To my amazing team, thanks for your hard work and dedication in helping bring my vision to life!

To my mentor. I am forever grateful to learning your principles. It has changed my life forever.

Foreword

The Prophet of Profit can and will alter your perception and transform your attitude about money and more specifically about profit.

As you dig into this book you will find profit is described as what is left after everything has been paid. Yet, in spite of the tremendous growth of self-help material over the past 50 years that is available to anyone who is genuinely interested in improving their personal situation the masses experience virtually no growth in profit but tremendous growth in debt. You might ask yourself "why is this so?" Then take a real honest look at your own situation.

Has your income and profit grown substantially each year
or are you finding that in spite of your best efforts, year after year,
your results are much the same?

There is a definite reason for this. And as you go from page to page, the solution to this dilemma will begin to reveal itself. The beautiful truth about this book is that it contains the merit of simplicity. Anyone who has a sincere desire to enjoy an honest profit at the end of a given period of time, will learn how that can be accomplished.

There are many definitions that you can find for the word *Prophet*. I believe the definition I have found that best describes Jacquelyn MacKenzie as a *Prophet* is: a person who through the use of universal law can accurately predict the future. Study her book or go to one of her live classes. Do exactly what this *Prophet* suggests. You will learn how to accurately predict your future and your profits will continue to grow.

Jacquelyn has represented our company, The Proctor Gallagher Institute for the past several years. She has done excellent work for small to medium size businesses and individuals all over North America. I have been involved in personal development for well over 50 years. I have been friends with and associated with many very effective individuals in this industry but I have not met anyone who has taken the laws of success and shared them with others in a more effective manner.

Read every word in this book and then go back and read it over again. But before you start activate your imagination and answer this question:

**What would my life look like if
I were living exactly the way I want to live?**

Don't be shy. This book, coupled with Jacquelyn's assistance will help you turn your most beautiful image into results.

I have spoken with a number of people that Jacquelyn has worked with and in every case, they are quick to tell me… this woman is without question a *Prophet of Profit*. That's because she is a product of her own product and she cares… she truly cares. AND she is an excellent communicator of the material which is very important!

Sandra Gallagher and I are very proud to have her and her company representing Proctor Gallagher Institute. What you are holding in your hands could literally change your life. Reading and memorizing this book will be of no help to you. Understanding and applying these ideas will be the key to achieving the life of your dreams. Make these ideas that you're receiving from the *Prophet of Profit* a part of your way of thinking; a part of your way of life.

Bob Proctor

Contents

Chapter 1

Profit is an Honorable Word

A prophet is a person who is delivering good news, and I want you to understand this... Profit is an honorable word. This word should be added to your vocabulary whether you are a business owner, an entrepreneur, a stay at home mom or someone working for a company; it doesn't matter to me. The word is "profit."

This word is so important, yet it is not talked about nearly enough and not given the attention it truly deserves. There are things you want to be doing whether it's expanding your business or maybe on a personal level, you want to go on more vacations, and the number one reason that is getting in your way is this word: profit. There simply isn't enough.

What I am about to share with you, we were not taught in school. I certainly wasn't. I am of the opinion now that profit is something that should become a top priority in everyone's personal and professional life. This is why 1% of the population earns most of the money in the world! And unfortunately, the average individual does not understand how they are doing it. These people know something that the vast majority of the population doesn't. They know how to earn a profit. The principles that I am going to outline in this book have put me in the 1% of income earners in a few short years!

One of the biggest stresses people have is about money. They have no money, and there is nothing left over at the end of the month to do what they want to do. And worse, some have over spent and maxed everything out. Businesses are short on cash flow, and they are not able to expand their services. You see, everyone wants more: more money, more things, more trips, bigger houses, nicer cars, etc.… That is natural. We should want more, but I am going to be really honest with you – if this is you, and you are struggling with money, then something needs to change quickly because if you don't change it right now, then you are going to continue on the path you are on. And the reality is, it doesn't get better. It will get worse.

Profit, the dictionary describes it as *"A financial gain, especially the difference between the amount earned and the amount spent in buying, operating, or producing something."*

Now, what is money? Money is a current medium of exchange, and profit is the money that is left over after all of the expenses are paid out.

We are used to thinking of profit as what a business earns. Every company is in business to make a profit. This is why you start a business because you want to provide a service by helping people, and in return for the service, you earn money. Without ensuring you are earning a profit in your business, you can go out of business.

What about the profit in your personal finances? What is left over after you have paid all of your living expenses? Profit does not just apply to business; it also should apply to your personal finances. Profit is what allows you to do the things you want to do. And if there isn't a lot left over, then you might feel restricted in what you can do. It can be frustrating if money is what is holding you back. However, I have news for you. You can change all of this starting right now by taking control and by making it a top priority. That is what I did. I took control.

If you want to increase your personal income or increase the bottom line in your business or company, then profit needs to become a priority. You need to treat it with the importance it deserves.

Profit is the FIRST order of business! End of story.

There are three things you can start to do right now:

First, I want you to be extremely comfortable talking and thinking about money — the thought might scare you or make you uncomfortable right now —but the more you talk about it and think about it, the more you are going to start to understand it. Most people grow up not talking about money, learning how to use it, or worse yet, how to earn it and keep earning it. People who have money are comfortable with it and are comfortable spending it; so they continue to make more of it. They don't talk about it in a conceited or egotistical way; they are comfortable with it. They understand money. They know where it is. They know how to keep it and how to make more of it. Profit is a priority for them.

Second, don't ask for advice from your friends or people that have no money. They are the wrong people to ask. Why? Because they have no money! This second point is very important. If you want more money, then you want to have conversations or hang around people with more money than you. They are doing something that is working. Those are the people you want to follow or get advice from. The rule of thumb is, if they don't have what you want, then don't ask them.

Third, no more thinking that money isn't everything and that it can't buy happiness. I agree it can't completely buy happiness, but when you don't have to worry about money, you can enjoy life so much more and truly live the way you want. Just because you don't have the amount of money you want or need doesn't mean that wanting more money is wrong. The "wanting" part is a desire, and we are supposed to want more. We are here to enjoy life. "Wanting" more is what helps us grow.

Money is so important, and it deserves more positive attention than it typically gets. It pays for the roof over our heads, the food on our table, the clothing in our closet, and our needs and wants. Having the money you want, when you want, allows you to do the things you want to do. Without it, you can't go very far, and you will feel like you are handcuffed.

Without money, you can't live well in North America. To live in North America, or where ever you are located, it costs money and a lot of it. I know you know this, but what I'm trying to do is open up your mind to start thinking about this issue differently. Thinking about how important money is in your life and about all of the great things it is already providing you so that I can get you to see how important it really is.

How do you think about the money you are using to pay your bills? Are you dreading paying the bill or upset that the company is calling you to collect their money?

I want you to look at it this way if this is you. When you pay your bills, you are also supporting businesses that employ other people. People that you may know. For example, if the phone company is calling you, the person on the other end of the line is earning a salary or a wage from that company so that they can pay for the lifestyle they choose. You are also helping this company stay in business, which then is helping the people that work for them earn a living.

Spending money is also a good thing, whether you are paying your phone bill or paying for new furniture. The money that you are using is an exchange for the service that you used, and when you pay them for that service, it is helping them! Money is meant to be kept in circulation.

I want you to think about your money for a moment, whether it's in your business or your personal finances. Are you able to do the things you want to do? Perhaps it's expanding your products or services in your business, or on a personal level, maybe you want to travel more or buy your dream house. Are you able to do these things? Or do you wish you could do them, but you can't because there just isn't enough left over at the end of the month?

I now think about this and money all the time, but it took someone to teach me about the importance of money, how I looked at money and what it meant to me before I really got it. I can assure you this – if you want more money, then you need to spend some time understanding it and understanding what it means to you and how money is affecting your life.

Now the truth is, most people are always thinking about money, but unfortunately, they are thinking about it in a negative way. The lack of money they have, the debt they have, the shortage of money, not being able to do what they want when they want, the struggle they are feeling with their money, and the list could go on.

Money is used for two things:

1. To make us comfortable (whatever the comfort level is for you) and

2. To extend our good far beyond our own presence.

Now isn't that a beautiful way to think about money?

Now you may be saying to yourself, *How do I extend it far beyond my own presence when I don't have any extra money?*

Well, let's first start by adding the word "profit" to your finances. Remember, profit is the amount of money left over after you've paid all of your expenses.

At the moment, your profit, or your money left over, may be one of four th.

1. A lot left over
2. A little left over
3. None left over or
4. A deficit (you owe more than what you are currently bringing in)

If you fall between 2 and 4, it's okay! I've been there.

Whatever your current situation is, it's a glimpse of where you currently are in your finances. It doesn't have to be where you are headed because you have a choice and can change all of it right now if you choose. When you allow yourself to stay focused on your current situation, that is going to keep you stuck because you won't be able to see your way out. You will continue only to see lack and limitation and what you don't have.

Here is a simple rule. If you focus on debt, you will stay in debt.

Next, I want you to let go of the past. Your past mistakes, things that you've been holding on to. Let go of how you got to where you are, wishing you had done it differently, wishing you could go back and do it again. Thinking this way does not serve you. It is impossible to go back and do it again, but what you can do is move forward with a greater understanding.

Think of it this way: your past is only an indication of where you've been. If you start to look back on your life, you will see a pattern. The reason it hasn't changed is because you haven't done anything differently to change the pattern or have not stayed consistent with it, and it hasn't been a priority to change it in your life. You can say, "Well, I have tried to change it." Trying is not enough.

I've made a ton of mistakes too, everyone has, but I've realized that those mistakes are how we learn. It's how I learned, and it's how you are learning, and if you ask any successful person, they too have made a ton of mistakes. The only difference is they don't let their mistakes take them down. They look at it completely different. They look at challenges and their mistakes as an opportunity to learn and grow. The only thing that matters at this point is you wanting to change all of this. This is what I want you to begin to focus on. Change your focus from where you currently are and then ask yourself what you would like to happen?

You have a really important decision to make. What are you going to do with the rest of your life? We are here for only a short period, and you have to make a decision that it stops here. That you deserve more because you do deserve more.

You have the power to choose right now to change your situation no matter what it is. But first I want you to ask yourself a question:

Am I ready to change and improve my finances?

If the answer is no, then you can continue to read, but nothing is going to change, and you are going to continue on the same path you are on.

However, if your answer is yes, then I want you to get really serious, make the decision, and commit to yourself to doing this. No matter what!

Here's the harsh reality. There is no magic pill. I can't do it for you. No one can do it for you. But you can do it for yourself. I can give you all the tips and tools, but until you decide to commit to your decision and take action, nothing is going to happen. Reading this book is not going to make you a profit or increase your income, but what you do with the information I am going to share with you will.

Also, I want to make this clear. This isn't something that is going to happen overnight or fall out of the sky. I want you to add another word to your vocabulary. Patience! Don't let impatience overwhelm you and say to you, "It's not working!" It will work, but you have to let it work. Carrot seeds do not grow overnight. They need water and nurturing. Next, wishing for things to get better will not make them better.

Again, I realize you may be thinking, "I know what you are saying right now," but I'm going to be honest with you... You think you know, but you don't. Don't undermine the simplicity of what I'm telling you.

The truth is, knowing is not enough. Knowing is not going to improve anything. What you know and what you do are two completely different things. It's going to take some work and commitment on your end, but if you stick with me, you will need a telescope when you look back on this moment! How do I know this? Because I live it every day. I feel like I need a telescope when I look back at how much has changed for me. I've accomplished more in the last couple of years than I ever have. The bottom line is, I've turned my life around, increased my income to be in the 1% of income earners, and I help other people every day do the same thing.

I have a client who is a very respected lawyer in his field, and I was working with him and his whole team. Not only did the culture of his company change, but the bottom line in his company also increased eight times in three months! I have many other clients that have done the same thing. As you keep reading this book, you are going to understand why and how it changed.

In the previous pages, I said your profit is one of four things. Now get out your current statements or budget and take a look at it. How much is left over after all expenses are paid? Whether you have a lot left over or a little, chances are you want to keep increasing it. There are likely things you want to be doing that you are currently not able to do because you need more money.

I have worked with individuals who are very successful, earning millions of dollars, and you know what? They want to keep increasing their income too. Why? Because they still have things they want to achieve or improve. Having more money allows you to extend your service beyond your physical presence. Without it, you are not able to reach as far.

What are some of your beliefs around money? What were you taught? Let me ask you this, and I want you to be honest with yourself. Are you someone who looks at the price before you decide to do something? Are you someone who goes straight to the sales rack and that becomes your selection? Are you someone who dreams of going on that vacation or buying a house or car? Are you someone who wants to give to charity or start your own foundation? Are you someone who wants to start your own business, or are you someone who wants to quit your current job?

The number one reason that is stopping you from doing what you want to do is, let me guess, money? Money is what stops most people from doing the things they really what to do. Therefore, if you want to start doing what you want to do, you need to increase the profit in your income.

So now my question is… are you ready to do this? Are you ready to take control? Are you ready to go after what you really want?

Okay, then let's start!

Chapter 2

Tell Me What You Want
and I'll Show You How to Get It

There are three important things you need to know, and they are:

1. Where you are
2. Where you are going and
3. What's holding you back

This is so simple but so easily missed because of the simplicity of it.

First, where you are. This is so important. If you don't know where you are in your current financial situation, then how will you be able to change it? In Chapter 1, I wanted to open up your mind to get you thinking about what you are currently earning and what your results were showing you. Be honest with yourself. I meet with all types of people. Some tell me exactly what's going on. Then I also meet people that tell me that their income is good; they dress nice, drive a nice car, and live in a nice house, but they have no money. They are maxed out. Something is definitely wrong there.

It's simple; your current financial results are either one of two things, positive or negative. There are no in-betweens, and they can't be both at the same time.

For now, let's treat your current financial results like a report card you get in school. It's a report on how well you are doing. If this were a test, and you wanted to get a better grade on the next test, what would you do, or what do you think you should do to improve your grade? You would study!

What kind of grade would you give yourself when you look at your financial situation? This grade is only a reflection of what your current financial results are. For example, when you were in school, and you received a bad mark in math, the mark you were given was only a reflection of where your level of consciousness was at that time. Fast forward to now. I bet if you retook the test, you'd get 100%. You know so much more now than you knew when you were younger.

This works the same way when it comes to your finances. Once you know, you can improve it. Now what happens to some people is the "report card" can take a person down. You look at it, and if it's really bad, you start to think all kinds of things like, "I'm never going to get out of this. I'm too much in debt. I can't seem to get ahead. I never have any money. How did I allow this to happen? Why didn't I know better? And so on. It can stir up all these emotions of stress, fear, doubts and worries, and this can make you feel stuck, like there is no way out.

How do you get out of this? As I mentioned earlier, you want to study. Study what? you ask. Study you. Find out why you keep getting the same results over and over again and why you are stuck. The reason you are where you are right now is because of you. You want to find out why your income isn't improving and why your profit isn't growing. And the reason you may think your income isn't improving isn't the real reason. The real reason is in you.

Study is something most people don't want to do, especially the studying I am suggesting, because we were not taught to study ourselves. We were taught to look to the outside for solutions, for things in our circumstance to change first, to ask other people what their thoughts or opinions are, or what they think we should do. And because of this, every time we are stuck, we don't know how to get ourselves unstuck. The answer to your problems lies within you.

Opinions are the cheapest commodity on earth! Everyone has one! I heard this once from my mentor, and I tend to agree with him. Stop asking people what they think you should be doing. Everyone has an opinion of what you should be doing, and the truth is, you already know what to do; however, there are things getting in your way that are stopping you from knowing, such as belief and confidence in yourself.

Here is a simple exercise to help you find the answer to a situation. Pretend a friend or a colleague is coming to you for advice about your situation and they are asking you for help. What would you say to them? What would you tell them to do? I bet you would have all sorts of advice to give them. People have all kinds of advice for other people, but when it comes to themselves, they can't see solutions. All of a sudden, their mind goes blank. By doing this exercise, you are removing yourself from the situation as if it were happening to someone else, and now you can see what to do. It is always easier to see something in someone else than it is to see something in you. By doing this, you are now going within for the answer!

What you are starting to do is "think." You are thinking about your situation from a different perspective.

All leaders of our time agree on one thing. "We become what we think about." I suppose when I first heard this, I wasn't quite sure what it meant, but fast forward a couple of years, and I think about everything in my life completely different than I used to.

This was something very important that was taught to me by my mentor. He taught me how to really think about me, what I am doing, how I am doing it and always think about the direction I am going. Now, I am always looking at my current results. There is a great deal of power in this knowledge because it allows you to see what is happening. When you can see what is happening, you can change it, especially if what you are doing is not working. And if it is working, you still want to know this information because it gives you an opportunity to improve upon it.

The worst thing you can do is ignore your results, good or bad. They will not just go away or improve on their own. Unfortunately, as you know, this doesn't happen. In fact, the opposite happens; they get worse. Even if what you are doing is working temporarily, you have to keep improving upon what you are doing as you will eventually hit the "glass ceiling." Not able to get past a certain point. You want to keep stretching yourself.

The bottom line is, get into the habit of always looking at your results!

I want you to write out your current situation when it comes to money. Start by writing out what your current results are, the way they are, in all its negativity. An example might be, "My income is never consistent. One month I'm earning $5,000, and the next, I'm earning $3,000. I never have enough left over to put into savings or pay all of my bills; I am always behind. I'm not able to go on vacations. I'm going further and further into debt. I can't seem to increase my income. My credit cards are always maxed out. My income is staying the same…" That is an example of where you currently are.

When you look at your results, take responsibility for them, no matter how bad they are. There is so much power in just owning it because the truth of the matter is, you are responsible.

If you are getting positive results, you are responsible. If you are getting negative results, you are responsible. Don't be offended by this. There is empowerment in taking responsibility for your results, no matter what they are. We are responsible for our health, our happiness, our relationships and our wealth!

You are responsible for your income. You are responsible for the amount of income you earn. You are responsible for what you do with your income. You are responsible for the profit you are left over with at the end of the month. The list could go on, but you get the gist. Just own it and move on. Just take it as a learning experience. You are learning.

When you take responsibility, you are taking control of your results. When you pass the responsibility off or, in other words, blame your partner, your family, conditions or circumstances, you are giving these things all of the power. You are letting them control you. You take control by taking responsibility. When you take control, you can now point yourself in a new direction. The direction you want to go!

We just covered where you are by getting you to take a look at what your current results are showing you. Now, my next question to you is, *What do you really want?*

This is the hardest question for most people to answer, but it is the first question I ask everyone I meet with. If I'm meeting with a CEO or an individual, I always ask them what they want, where they want to go and what they want to achieve.

Most people are thinking of what they don't want rather than what they do want.

To answer this question, get out a pen and paper, sit down, totally relax, and begin to ask yourself a number of questions.

Start out by asking yourself:

What do I really want?

What do I want my life to look like?

What are some of the things I want to be doing?

What do I love to do?

What kind of income do I want to be earning?

When do I want to have this all by?

What kind of company do I want to have?

Where do I want to take my company?

What does my team of people look like?

Just start writing out whatever comes to your mind. Create a shopping list of what you want. This exercise will begin to open up your mind to start thinking. As you are writing things down, think from a place of: if you had all the money you needed, all the resources you needed, what would you be doing? What would your life look like?

This exercise might take a while as you are not accustomed to thinking this way. Give yourself some time to complete the exercise. You may receive thoughts while you're driving, in the shower, at work, cooking dinner; they will come to you when you are completely relaxed and open. Take note of them. I always tell my clients to get into the habit of taking a notebook with you wherever you are going, and if something occurs to you, write it down.

I will warn you, there is one thing that might get in your way, and that is "how." How is this going to happen? When you start thinking about the how, you are not going to see the "how" right away. Don't automatically reject the idea. Before this, you've probably been doing that already. It could be something you really want, but you shut it down right away because you don't know how, or you don't have the money, or you don't have the resources. That's okay; you don't need to know the how at this point. You just want to start thinking about what it is that you want.

Second thing, any time doubt or fear creeps into your mind, kick it out. It doesn't matter at this point. The only thing that matters is that we get you to start thinking about what you really want.

Once you have your list, start figuring what this is going to cost you. Create a budget. Yes, you read this right. I want you to create a budget for all of this. What does this lifestyle cost? Most people want more things; they want to travel more, shop more, save more, give more. They want to buy a bigger house or newer car, but they have no idea what any of this costs.

Treat this like your regular budget, but it is a budget based on how you want to live. The number that you come up with at the bottom is the income you need to earn to be able to afford this lifestyle.

Next, now that you've written out the way you want to be living, write it down. Start out by writing, *I am so happy and grateful now that…* and then write in the details of your goal, including the amount of money you need to be able to live this lifestyle, and then add a date when you would like to reach it by.

An example of your goal written out might be… *I am so happy and grateful now that I am earning $250,000 a year. I am living a life of freedom, traveling the world, and providing greater service to everyone.*

Why do you need to put an income and date on it? Because you have to make your goal measurable. Otherwise, how will you know when you've reached it? Also, saying that you want to be financially free is not enough. The words financially free can mean many different things. It could mean $20,000, $50,000, or it could mean $100. You have to be clear.

Most people I meet say they just want to be financially free. I have no idea what that number is to you, and more importantly, when you say this to yourself, you don't know what that number is. You need to know this number. The number you came up with when you did your "dream budget"; that is what financial freedom means to you.

We were not taught to do this. The sad thing is that most people are taught to lower their standard of living to match their current income level. What we should have been taught is to create our standard of living and raise our income level to match that standard of living, not the other way around.

If you are earning, $50,000, you were probably taught that is what your standard of living is. The bank says based on your salary, you can afford a mortgage of approximately $200,000, so you look at houses in this range. You do what we call "settle."

Take a look at what you are currently settling for. The way you are living right now is what you are settling for. Some of it might be good, and some of it not so good. You settle for whatever your employer gives you as a salary. You settle for whatever the bank tells you that you can afford. And you are settling for your current lifestyle, the way you are living, the number of things you have, the kinds of things you have.

Now, I want to make this clear; there are things that you are settling for that you love. That's great! That's not what I'm talking about. I'm talking about the things you are not happy with and the things you want to change. If you are not happy with something, this is what you are settling for. If you are not happy with your income, this is what you are settling for, and so on. If you are working for a company that you don't like, you are settling. In other words, you are choosing to live like this.

You might be saying to yourself, *Well, the company I work for controls how much I make.* Listen, your salary is delivered through your company, but it is you that controls how much you make. You might be an entrepreneur that says that the economy controls your income. The economy doesn't control your income; you control your income. If you want to earn more money in the company you are working for, then you need to start doing more than you are currently being paid for. If you do not do more than you are being paid for, you will never be paid for more than you are doing.

If your attitude is, pay me first and then I'll do it, you will not go very far. It doesn't work like that. Changing this alone will help you increase your income.

Once your goal is written out, carry it with you everywhere, and read it every day. This is the direction you are headed. As humans, we need direction. It's no different than getting into your car and driving to your destination. You wouldn't get into your car and say to yourself, I wonder where I should go. No, you get into your car because you have somewhere to be. Well, now I want you to start treating your life the same way. You have somewhere to be and a place that you are going. Treat your goal with the utmost respect and attention it deserves. This is your life; it is the direction you are headed. Protect it.

People spend more time planning their weekends and holidays and spend very little time planning their life and what they want to do with it. You might think about your life and things that you want to be doing at times, but it doesn't go any further than that. Put the same amount of attention and detail that you would put into your weekends or events into the planning of your life!

You have an important question to answer. *What are you going to do with the rest of your life?*

You are here for a short period. Why not do something great with the balance of the time left, and live the way you truly were designed to live?

If you are still having a hard time figuring out what you want, I always tell my clients that sometimes we don't know what we want because we haven't experienced that much. Get out there and experience different things, whether it's taking a class or trying something new and different. How do you know if you are going to like something if you haven't experienced it yet? I always find this interesting because sometimes, you will make up your mind before you've even tried it or say you are not interested or don't like it simply because you don't have the money to do it. I'm not talking about going and trying some disgusting food here. I'm talking about experiencing different things in life.

What do you love to do? I will tell you one thing; when you do what you love, it doesn't feel like work.

Once you have written down your goal and the income level you want to reach, I want you to ask yourself two questions:

1. *Are you able?* Yes, you are able because you are here, you are breathing, and you are alive. So the answer should be yes, I can go after my goal and increase my income.

2. *Are you willing?* Are you willing to do what it takes to get to your goal? The difference between people who don't reach their goal and the people who do reach their goal is that they are not willing to do what it takes. They give up at the first bump along the way, and they revert to what they were doing before.

You have to be willing to do what it takes. My mentor told me once, and he's right — there are no shortcuts to success. It doesn't happen overnight. It does not happen by chance or luck. It happens by design. You create it. You can create it. It happens to the people who are willing to do what it takes, willing to pay the price to get there. The willingness to overcome any challenges or obstacles that get in the way.

When you look at successful people, the people that are making it happen, you look at them where they are right then and there. As successful. You don't realize the journey it took for them to get there, what they went through to get to where they were going. But if you ask any of them, they are not going to tell you it happened by luck. They made it happen. And there were probably times they almost gave up, but they didn't. They kept going because they were so passionate about what they were doing that it was worth everything.

What they have done is developed the determination, discipline, and the persistence to keep going. Their desire to succeed was bigger than the challenges they faced.

They have developed a mental toughness and mental muscles. They have cultivated good habits. They spend time and money constantly investing in them, investing in mentors, spending time and money to better themselves, spending time and money developing their strengths, how to become better than they were yesterday, spending time and money figuring out who they are as a person.

What comes out of all this? Confidence. Confidence is knowledge. Knowledge of knowing one's self. They are confident because they know themselves. They are confident in their abilities to carry it out. They have great habits. They know how to create new habits when one is not working. They are very focused and productive individuals. They know that there is always a better way. The bottom line is, they know how to get results. That's why they are in the 1%. They are willing to do what it takes. This is why this group is so small.

They have also shut out all the naysayers. There are always going to be naysayers out there. People that tell you that you shouldn't do this: people who don't believe in your ideas. What they are really telling you is they don't believe they can do it. You have to develop the mental strength and toughness to tune all of that out because if you let their doubts creep into your mind, you're done. You will start believing what they are telling you.

As you embark on your goal, your circle of friends may change. They may stop talking to you, calling you, or texting you. I'm here to tell you it's normal; it's okay. Your friends and family are operating from a different way of thinking. They are not you. They are operating from their limiting beliefs.

Take a look at the five people you spend the most time with. These five people have the most direct influence on you. They will influence the way you think, your beliefs, your decisions, your opinions, and the direction your life is going. If you want to know your future, take a look at who you are spending the most time with. That is the hard truth. Your friends and family are good people, but they can also hold you back.

What will happen, though, when you make a decision to go after what you want, is you will attract new people who are on the same frequency as you or, in other words, the same level of thinking as you. They see your vision. They are in harmony with you and where you are going. You will attract people, resources, and opportunities to you. You want to surround yourself with creative and productive individuals who know where they are going.

I read something once that said to always hang around people who are smarter than you, have more money than you, and are overall more successful than you. As you surround yourself with these people, you will learn from them. When you learn from them, put what you learn into action right away. They know what works.

When you begin your journey to your goal, will you run into obstacles or challenges? Yes, absolutely, you will. And when you do, don't automatically think that you failed. Failure is only when you stop. All it means is that there was an error in the plan. Your plans can change. Your plans always change. If one way doesn't work, try a different way. I call this course correction. All you are doing is correcting your course. That's it. There is always a way to get to where you want to go. You just haven't thought of it yet. If it were easy, everyone would be doing it.

Thomas Edison failed 10,000 times before the light bulb was invented. As a child, his teacher and parents told him he would never succeed. Walt Disney was fired from a newspaper for the lack of imagination. JK Rowling's book was rejected numerous times before it hit fame. Look at Steve Jobs and the struggles he went through. People thought the Wright Brothers were crazy because they were trying to fly a plane in the air. Henry Ford failed in his business multiple times before Ford Motors was created. Oprah Winfrey, Michael Jordan, you've heard their stories. Study these people. Study successful people. You'll be astounded at what you find out, and you will learn something by studying them.

The point is, these people didn't give up. They've been through struggles, hardship, failed numerous times, and risked everything to get where they wanted to go. I love what Oprah said about failure *"There is no such thing as failure. Failure is just life trying to move us in another direction."*

I am now going to introduce a word to you that gets in your way and can hold you back from going after what you really want. This word is paradigm! If you do not know what this word means, then you have no idea how much it is impacting your life. It controls the amount of money you earn; it controls your health, your relationships, it controls everything. It controls what you see and what you believe to be true. This word is the reason you are stuck. It is this word that is keeping you from doing what you should be doing.

What is a paradigm? I love how Bob Proctor describes this word. A paradigm is a mental program that controls almost all of our behavior, and almost all of our behavior is habitual.

There are things that you are doing out of habit. You are doing things that you are giving no conscious thought to. For example, when you wake up, you follow a pattern in the morning. You aren't thinking about what you are doing. You just get up and follow your routine.

Well, the same can happen in your life. You are following a pattern. Probably a pattern you've done a few times that has led you to where you are, and you keep doing it because you have given it no conscious thought as to why.

Do you ever ask yourself, *Why does this always happen? Why does this keep happening?* It's because you are doing the same things over and over again, but the problem is, you are expecting different results each time you do it. You haven't changed what you are doing; therefore, you will continue to get the same results.

Definition of insanity, I know you know it! Doing the same thing over again but expecting different results. Everyone knows this, yet they continue to keep doing the same thing and then ask themselves, *Why? Why are things not improving?*

Sounds absurd, doesn't it? Like, why didn't I see this before? It is absurd. This is not rocket science, and it is not complicated. I've mentioned several times the simplicity of what I'm telling you. It's so simple, so obvious; however, the vast majority of people miss it.

The answer to all of this is you have to study. I'm going to keep saying it. Study doesn't just mean studying a new skill or taking a course. You can study you. As you study you, you are going to increase your conscious awareness. It's going to be like a light was turned on, and all of a sudden, you can see. All of a sudden, you can see what you are doing and why you are doing it.

You did not originate some of your beliefs and behaviors. They were passed along to you from generation to generation. Habits and behaviors that you have right now are other people's habits that you have adapted to. These beliefs and behaviors have so much control over what you do and how well you do things.

This mental programming is controlling your income. It's controlling your beliefs around money. What do you believe about money? Do you think money is hard to earn? I grew up believing three things: 1) money did not grow on trees, 2) money was hard to earn, and 3) you only buy something if you need it. These beliefs that you have control your behavior, which then controls the actions you take.

You are earning what you are earning because you are not programmed to earn what you really want to earn. What I am talking about can apply to every area of your life, but right now, we are talking about money.

Here is the good news: you can change the programming. It's what I did. I changed my programming. I changed my paradigm, and I am continuing to change my paradigm. The more I continue to work on me, change up what I'm doing and how I'm doing it, the more my income goes up!

Take the goal that you have come up with, get emotionally involved with it, and make up your mind you are going to do what it takes to get there!

Chapter 3

Make Room for Your New Bank Account

Clear out the old and make room for the new. In the previous chapter, you took a look at what your current results were showing you. Then you created your goal based on the way you want to live, and I introduced a word to you. That word was paradigm. Remember that a paradigm is a multitude of habits and behaviors.

Let's take a look at some of your habits and behaviors when it comes to money. First and foremost, how about your spending habits? Everyone wants more. Maybe it's a bigger house, new furniture or going on vacations. Wanting "more" is a good thing. However, there is something huge that is missing.

You are not doing anything to increase your income so you can afford some of those wants and desires. Therefore, credit cards become maxed out. You've got the nice house, the nice car, but you've stretched yourself so thin that your income doesn't cover everything. This is a huge problem, and I meet people all the time that are in this situation. This may be you, or you may know people in similar situations.

What does this do? It creates worries, doubts, fears, stress and anxiety. Sound familiar?

You can have all of the things that you want more of; I think you should have more of them if that is what you want. But you need to do something to increase your bottom line, the profit part. Remember, profit is the amount of money left over after all the expenses are paid. Work at increasing that number!

I'm going to go back to an extremely important point here.

Create your standard of living, whatever that number is. If it's higher than what you are currently bringing in, then you need to raise your income level to match your standard of living. It's that simple.

Don't give yourself the excuse, *Yeah, but you don't understand, My company controls how much I make. They won't give me a raise. I work 40+ hours a week, and I don't have any more time.*

These are what we call "excuses" and alibis. Don't let your excuses control why you can't do something. This is where you have to make a decision, a really important one. What is it that you are going to sacrifice in order to get what it is you want?

If you keep doing what you are currently doing, what is going to be the result? If it hasn't changed by now, then chances are it's not going to until you make the decision to change some habits and behaviors that are controlling you. Change always happens with you first. When you change you, your results will change.

If what you are doing is not working, stop doing it. It's simple. Don't make it more complicated than it has to be.

I'm just being honest with you. Don't be offended. Honesty is what got me moving in the right direction. It can be hard to hear or to face at times, but it's the only way. My mentor told me in the beginning that if your way is not working, then why don't you try my way? And now, it's what I, in turn, teach my clients. I teach them the way that I have learned. As a result of this, my income has changed along with my clients' income. Because to change anything in your life, you have to start with you first.

By studying you, you will understand how you operate, how you function, what makes you tick, what your strengths are, and what are some of the habits and behaviors that are sabotaging your success. And to do this, you will need to spend some time understanding the mind. Your mind is the most powerful resource you have. Because everything starts in your mind.

There is a part of your mind that needs to be changed for your results to change.

When you first think of your mind, you automatically think of your brain. The truth is, no one has ever seen the mind. Mind is in every cell of your body. Mind is what controls your body. It controls the movement of your body.

We have two parts to our mind. First, we have our conscious mind where we take in and gather information through our five senses by what we see, hear, taste, touch, and smell.

It is this part of the mind where we store information from the experiences and knowledge we've gained. This is the "knowing" part of the mind. As you are reading this book, you are gathering information. This is also the part of the mind that we do our thinking from. Thoughts and ideas flow in and out of your conscious mind. It's where ideas originate. It is this part of the mind that you created your goal from.

The second part to your mind is called the subconscious mind. This is the part of the mind that controls your actions or simply put this is the "doing" part of the mind. What controls your actions? Your behavior controls your actions. And your habits control your behavior. Your subconscious mind is in control of what you do and how well you do it.

This part of the mind needs to be changed to create better results. The things you are doing right now, you are programmed to do. You don't even know why you do some of the things you are doing. And this is where your paradigm is stored. It is stored in a section of your subconscious mind.

For you to increase your income and create your new way of living, you will need to study this. You will want to know how you are programmed. You will want to know what you are not doing what you should be doing. What are some things that you are doing that continue to get in your way?

For example, a lot of people struggle with procrastination, discipline, focus, fear of criticism, confidence and the list goes on. These are roadblocks. These are just some of the things that you need to improve.

Your habits and behaviors are going to be either positive or negative. You will have both. It is the negatives ones you want to change. You need to replace a negative habit with a positive habit. However, just becoming aware of your habits will not change anything.

So far I've just explained on an entry level how the mind functions, but for this to become a permanent change, you must begin with changing the way you currently think.

Thinking is the highest function we are capable of, and yet most people don't think. They think they think, but they don't. Mental activity does not constitute thinking. If you pay close attention to what people are saying or doing, you will soon see that they are not thinking; otherwise, they would never be doing what they do. A person would never intentionally do something that resulted in a negative outcome. They are just not thinking. Thinking it through. Thinking about the result. Thinking about if what they are doing is aligned with where they are going.

Remember when I said I think about money and profit all of the time? Well, I'm thinking about my goal which is essentially my income or my company's income. I'm thinking about what I need to bring in every month for me to live the lifestyle I want to live. I'm thinking about what I need to bring in every month to pay my team members and what I need to keep my business running and growing. I'm constantly thinking about money. Profit is the first order of business. Without focusing on and bringing in profit every month, you can get into trouble quickly.

If you have employees, this has to be at the forefront of your mind. You are responsible for paying their salary or wage and responsible for paying yourself. You are responsible for bringing in more business. If you don't have a business, you are still responsible for your income and making sure you have enough profit left over so you can live the way you want to live.

Knowing this is not enough. People will say they "know" a lot. People know all kinds of stuff, just like you know a lot as well. As I mentioned earlier, there is a huge difference between knowing and doing. We do not operate from the knowing part of our mind. We operate from the doing part of our mind, and that is our subconscious mind.

We've been taught to go on the premise that the more education we have, the more successful we will be. There are people who have degrees at the end of their name — they have a vast amount of information in their brain. But when you look at their results, they would indicate they don't know. They are getting poor results.

An education doesn't mean you will automatically be successful. It's what you do with the knowledge you have received from the education. It's the application of the knowledge through actions you take that determine your results. And your paradigm controls what you do with the knowledge you have. Your paradigm is in control of the "doing" and how well you do it.

Here's an example. Take the sales department in a company. Everyone in the department is given the same amount of training, everything to be successful and to become number one. They are given all of the tools and knowledge to succeed. One person is doing well and taking off like a rocket while other people are barely making it happen. Why is that?

Or think about network marketing, everyone knows someone who is in network marketing. They are all given the same amount of training and tools to be successful in their business, and there is typically only a small percentage of the entire company getting results. Why?

It is because they are not doing what they know how to do. They are not applying the information they have gathered. They are not applying what they are taught. It is because they are not programmed to do this. It can be really frustrating for people because they know they should be doing it, but they still are not doing it.

We were taught to operate based on intellect, how much we know. Companies will spend thousands of dollars teaching their people to know more. Teaching them how to sell more, how to close better, how to do presentations, etc.... It does not matter how much knowledge you have if you do not learn how to apply and take action on what you already know. Your paradigm is in control of the application of your knowledge. Without proper application, nothing happens.

Some examples that get in the way of application are fear, lack of confidence, discipline, and procrastination. I've mentioned these before, but these things hold so many people back from really making it happen. This is why studying you is so important. You can make minor shifts in the way you do things and just by doing this you will see a dramatic increase in your results.

Think for a moment about how much knowledge and experience you have right now. Chances are you already know what to do to improve your income or your business. You know what needs to be done, but you are still not doing it.

This can cause a lot of frustration and confusion because there is part of you that is saying to yourself, *Why can't I do this? Why can't I get ahead? Why can't I make this sale?*

What then happens is that we justify these questions with something like this, *Well, the economy is down. I don't have enough time. There isn't enough business. My boss doesn't like me. I'd better get more sales training. I'd better invest in more marketing. I need to go and take this course, etc.*

I'm not saying this is not important, but if you do not get to the root of the problem of why you are not doing what you already know you should do, nothing will change. You will spend more money, waste more time getting more knowledge, and you will still be stuck. I see this all the time, and you know what? I used to be that person. That person was continually getting stuck. Nothing changed until I decided to change what I was doing and how I was doing it.

I was speaking with a client, and their entire team, whom I had been working with for the past five months. I asked them how things had changed since we started. They replied that since their team changed their way of thinking and the way they were doing things (they were changing their programming), the business increased ten times in five months! They are attracting huge opportunities for their company and are being recognized as leaders in their industry. Other companies want to work with them. What they are doing as a company is bringing out the best in their team by changing the programming. Changing the way they do things and how they do it. They have an amazing team, which is passionate about what they are doing and who all believe in where the company is going. All they are doing is studying, studying themselves, and how to do better than what they were previously doing.

If you want to dramatically increase your income and profits, then you will need to start studying. You want to study you, in a way, so you can learn how to become more effective, more productive, more disciplined, and stretch your thinking outside of the box.

This is something most people don't want to do. It's going to require some time, some money perhaps, and commitment on your end, but I'm going to tell you, if you do, you will be amazed at what will happen. This is exactly what I started to do that put me in the 1% of income earners. I started to study. And what I'm studying is me.

You are the only one who can improve your business, your situation, your income, and the direction you want your life to go in. Only you.

Pretend that it is the end of the year, and you are looking back. How much will your life improve or change by you reaching your goal? I bet it would change drastically! Well, for you to change it, you have to start with yourself. What you did last year is not going to be enough.

Chapter 4

I Know Where the Money Is

Let's raise your income level to match your new standard of living! That's exactly what I want you to focus on: how to raise your income level or how to increase the profit in your business.

Now you need to understand that the money you need is already here. I know what you are thinking right now! You're thinking, *Yeah, but I don't see it. Where is it?*

You are not going to see it until you actively start looking for it! What I mean by actively start looking for it is that you want to be thinking about earning more money.

You will need to increase your awareness about money and earning more money. What exactly does increase your awareness mean?

Here is an example. It wasn't that long ago that when we wanted to phone someone, we had to use the phones that were plugged into a wall in our home or office, and if we were outside of the house and needed to call someone, we had to stop by a pay phone. Hard to imagine that's what we had to do, but we did. Now we carry our phones with us everywhere we go.

Look at how things have changed since then. We have cell phones that are like mini computers and most people's office. You see, cell phones were always here, but it took people to become aware of how to improve upon what currently existed. They took the existing phone and made it better. What they did was raise their level of awareness as to how to accomplish this. As a result of this, we can communicate with people around the world by using just our cell phone. As "people" continue to improve upon an idea, they became aware of how to make it better.

When it comes to money, it works the same way. If you want to add more income or profit to your bottom line, then you need to increase your awareness around money and provide greater service. Improve upon what you are currently doing. Provide more service. You have to provide something in exchange for money. You need to give something to get something. You will not be able to increase your income without providing something in exchange for the income you will receive.

Let's get into what you are thinking about right now because your thoughts are related to your level of awareness.

Are you focused on the lack of money and reasons you can't increase your income level? This is a really important point because if that is what you are thinking and what you are focused on, that is the only thing you are going see. You are going to see lack and limitations.

To increase the profit in your business or the profit in your personal finances, you want to think about how you can add more money, what you can be doing to add more service, provide more value, how to do it better. Think how you can improve what you are already doing.

When you are thinking this way, what you are doing is increasing your level awareness, to adding more. Do you see the difference already? Try it for a moment. Stop and ask yourself how you can increase your income right now, how you can increase the profits in your business. I bet you have a few ideas already!

There are thousands of opportunities surrounding you right now, but if you are not thinking opportunities, then you won't see them. Whatever you are thinking is what you are going to see. Pretty simple.

You see, there was a time when I couldn't see very far. I could only see what was directly in front of me. I could only see what my present results were showing me, and it was keeping me stuck because I kept focusing on them, focusing on lack. That's all I saw. This changed when I began to really "think." When you begin to think, you see things differently.

What is awareness, exactly? Awareness (as described by Wikipedia) is *the state or quality of being conscious of something*. When you are conscious of it, you are aware of it. Awareness is having knowledge about something.

Think about this for a moment. There is someone out there right now that is currently earning what you want to be earning. They are doing what you want to be doing. They are selling the same products or services, and they are doing well. The only difference is, they are aware of something that you are not aware of. They are aware of how to do it and how to do it well. That's it. They have knowledge that you don't.

I want you to think of your awareness as it applies to you and your present results. Better yet, your financial results; your results are in direct ratio to where your current level of awareness is. That is what you are consciously aware of at this present moment. It's what you currently know how to do.

Your current income is your awareness level. You know how to earn what you are earning right now. Someone who is earning $50,000 a year is not thinking the same as someone who is earning $100,000 or $300,000 and vice versa. They are operating from a completely different level of awareness. Your income is in direct proportion to what you are presently thinking.

This applies to everything you are doing; however, we are only talking about money at this particular time because I know that is what you really want to know how to do!

Simply put, if you are not earning the income that you want, then you need to increase your awareness around money: becoming comfortable with it, understanding it, understanding that what you are looking for is already here, understanding how to earn it, how to keep it and how to keep increasing it.

You want to be thinking of how to do better than what you are currently doing. We can always do better than what we are doing now because there is always a better way to do everything. The best way has not yet been discovered. When you relate this to your business or your personal finances, ask yourself how you can do better than what you are currently doing. As you focus on this, this will increase the ideas coming to you. Now you want to act on those ideas and not dismiss them, as these are the answers you are waiting for. A closed mind cannot accept new ideas; an open mind can accept any new idea. If you are locked in by what your current results are showing you, you will reject any idea or answers you are waiting for. This is why it is so important to understand your mind, how it functions, and how powerful it is.

Where does all of this go? Right to the bottom line. Profit. Profit allows you to do things beyond what you are doing at the moment. It might be expanding your business or your team, or it might be on a personal level where you are traveling more or buying your dream house. If you want to do this right, meaning make this a permanent change, then you will need to invest some time understanding your mind.

You may want more money. You may want to increase your income level. But the "wanting" part will not change anything. Just because you want it doesn't mean it will change.

Think about this for a moment. Stop and think about what you are doing. Stop and think about the things you are thinking about. If you are unsure, take a look at your results. Your results will show you what you've been thinking about. Positive or negative, it's what you've been thinking about.

Thinking is the highest function we are capable of. Everything starts from the thoughts you are thinking. Your results are a reflection of the things you are thinking and feeling. How does this relate to your level of awareness? You need to start thinking of something new. As you start thinking of it, you are going to increase your level of awareness, and you will start to see where the opportunities are.

Here is a simple example that you can relate to. Pretend you are having a conversation with a friend, and they are talking about getting a new car that you've never seen or heard of before. You leave the conversation, and all of a sudden, you see that exact car everywhere. It's driving beside you, in the parking lot, and you begin to see it everywhere. You see, it was always there. You just weren't aware of it before.

Here is another example of awareness. Take a baby, for instance. They are not aware of the difference between a man and a women. They are not born knowing the difference. They become aware of the difference as they learn.

How do you increase your level of awareness? Through study. It's the only way. You are going to hear me say this over and over again: you have to study. You have to develop understanding. Start by studying yourself. You are the problem; even better, you are the solution to all of your problems. Once you start to study yourself, you will see things so differently. You will start to see you are capable of doing what you want to be doing in the process.

There are so many opportunities around you right now. We live in a world full of them. What are you looking for? Are you looking for opportunities, or are you looking at your limitations and what you don't have? There is a huge difference between the two. If you want to increase your income, start thinking about money. When you think about earning more money, you are going to get ideas.

What do you do with those ideas?

Most of the time, you probably don't do anything with them. Do you know how many great ideas you've probably had that you have dismissed, just like that? Yet you keep asking for help, asking for answers. You are getting all the answers you need; they are coming to you in the form of ideas, and you are rejecting them before you give them any second thought.

The money you need is already here. You are just not aware of where it is yet. When you increase your awareness in regards to money, you will start to see where it is. It is already here. When I began to study, everything changed in my life. I now look at life completely different than I used to. And as a result of this, the things in my life changed. All I see now is endless opportunity, and it's exciting when you train yourself to look at life this way.

When I changed the way I looked at things, the things I looked at changed. My income has changed. The only difference between two people where one person is getting desired results and the other isn't is they are aware of things that you are not. They are aware of how to do it.

I know right now if this is the first time you are hearing this, it might take you a bit of time to understand exactly what I mean, but just toy with this idea for a moment and really think about it. When I first heard it too, I had to really think about it and how I related to it and develop an understanding.

When I began to study this, my mentor taught me that everything we need is already here, and you can take your annual income and turn it into your monthly income. When he first told me this, I wasn't sure if I believed that, but I knew he believed it, and that was enough for me. Now, I believe it because that's what has happened to me. I turned my annual income into my monthly income. I know where the money is, and I know that everything I need is already here.

To do this, you want to work on developing your mindset around this. If this is the first time you are reading about this, I would go back and read it again. Reading something once or even twice does not mean you know it. You have to internalize what you are reading and relate it to you, so you understand.

Begin to spend your time thinking of ways you can increase your income or increase the profit. Take your new desired income level, write it on a piece of paper, and only write out ways you can make this happen. Any time a reason why it won't work enters your mind, reject it right away. Successful people do not spend time thinking of reasons why it can't be done, giving themselves excuses, or blaming outside circumstances or conditions for where they are. They spend all of their energy thinking of ways it can be done. They spend time developing the faculties of their mind. They spend time developing habits and behaviors that are getting in their way.

Do you know how many ideas you are receiving right now, every day, and are rejecting at the same time? A lot! Why are you rejecting them? Because your beliefs and behaviors are not in harmony with the ideas you are thinking. Therefore, you are rejecting them right away.

Financial success has a lot to do with being in the right place at the right time, and the only thing that is missing is your awareness. You are not aware that you are in the right place at the right time because you can only see what is not there. You are looking for the wrong thing. You are focused on circumstances.

The opportunities around you are limitless. The only thing that is blocking you from seeing them is you and your beliefs. You are looking for the big colorful flag, the billboard sign to tell you it's over here when this whole time, what you are looking for has been right in front of you.

These could be people, conversations, opportunities. Everything you need to get to your goal is already here, but if you are going by what you see, you are not going to get it. You want to develop your mental toughness, your persistence, your focus, develop your mind and cultivate an understanding.

How does this relate to increasing your income? It has everything to do with raising your income. Pay attention to what is going on around you.

You will attract everything you need, but you have to be aware of it when it's in front of you or you will miss it.

I bet you have had an opportunity right in front of you, but at the time, you were not aware of how great it was because you were letting skepticism, fear, and doubt get in the way. It was talking you out of doing it. It was justifying why you shouldn't do it. Why you should stay where you are and play it safe.

You couldn't see beyond that. You couldn't see the whole path ahead. You've never been there before; you've never done it before. Even though a part of you wanted to do it, you rejected it before you even gave it a second thought. You just talked yourself out of it. Looking back, maybe now you're saying, *Damn, I was there. I was talking to that person. I can't believe I didn't do it.*

How many times do you think you do this to yourself? Or how many times have you thought of an idea and didn't act on it, only to find out down the road that someone else had the same idea, and the only difference is they acted on it. Only you will know for sure, but I'm guessing a lot, more than you know. How many times do you talk yourself out of doing something because of something you've heard, something you've seen, something you've never done before, or simply because you didn't have the money or time to do it?

Raise your level of awareness by beginning to think larger than you are right now, by looking for opportunities. Only give your attention and thoughts to how it can be done. You will start to see them!

Chapter 5

Raise Your Income

Raising your income can be a simple concept if you let it, or it can be daunting if you've never done it before or feel like you're hitting a roadblock.

The number that you came up with when you created your "ideal" budget in the previous chapter is the number you want to work toward. Raising your income or profit to that number is going to allow you to live more comfortably and do the things you want to do.

If you are someone who is spending more than you make each month, you especially need to take this seriously. The only way to get out of the position you are in is to increase your income or profit. If you don't, nothing will change except you'll go further and further into debt, and all that does is cause unnecessary stress, worries, and frustration.

When you don't have to worry about money, you are so much more creative, but when you are worried about money, that is blocking your creative faculties, and your focus and energy are on the lack of money.

Therefore, the first thing I want to talk to you about is sales. Sales is the highest paid profession there is, but it can also be the lowest paid profession.

The reason it can be the lowest is those people do not spend any time developing themselves and getting better, so they don't make a lot of money, while the top sales professionals are always developing themselves, working on themselves, working at getting better than they were yesterday. They are mastering what it is they do.

Now you might be saying to yourself, I'm not in sales. I'm not a salesperson. Let's get this straight. Everyone is in sales, whether you admit it or not. If you are in business, you are in sales. If you are a one-man show, you are in sales; if you have your own store, you are in sales; if you are in network marketing, you are in sales; if you are in retail, you are in sales.

You are always selling something, whether it's a product, a service, or an idea.

There is such a stigma around being a salesperson. You don't want to be known as "someone selling something." What will people think if they know you are trying to sell them something? Even though you are in sales, you still might stay clear of salespeople because you don't want to be sold something. So right there – I would change your beliefs around salespeople. If you want to test drive a car, you have to go through a salesperson.

You cannot buy anything without going through the sales department. Every business, every company has to have a sales department. Without sales in a business, you cannot sell your products or services and, more importantly, you cannot earn a profit without it. If it is only you in your business, you are the sales department.

The first thing you need to do is change your perception around sales and the concept of a salesperson. Making a sale is a transaction between two people for some product or service. Salespeople generally get paid on commission, and the more they sell, the more they make. Why is being in sales the highest paid profession? Because your income can be unlimited! You are in charge of how much you make, and that is measured totally on you and your performance. It's not the product, not the company; it's all on you. How well you sell. Selling is leading someone into a path of agreement. Being in sales is helping people get what they want.

If you are an entrepreneur in business for yourself, take this seriously. Now you might be saying, *Of course, I know this*, but I meet so many people who are in sales, yet they have a negative concept around salespeople, and they don't want to be referred to as a "salesperson." If this is you, and you are struggling in sales, then you need to do some work on this. You see, it doesn't matter what product, widget, or service you have; you need to sell it first. You cannot help the person, company, etc., until you sell them something. Until you sell them on how what you have to offer is going to help them.

I often hear this from people when they get into business for themselves. It may be network marketing, or selling jewelry, insurance, houses or whatever it is, they are selling. They are scared to talk to people about what they have to offer. They are scared to talk to their friends about what they are doing. They are a "closet" salesperson.

This is one of the biggest things that hold people back from really making it happen. They fear criticism of what other people will think now that they are "selling something," especially when they first start out. When you first start in business, typically the first people you want to talk to about what you are doing are your friends and family.

In my opinion, this is the worst place to start. I'm not saying don't tell them what you are doing; just don't sell to them. They don't see you as this person yet. They don't see the value in what you are doing because nothing has happened yet. Friends and family almost need to see you become successful at what you're doing before they take you seriously.

What happens is, this can really mess with your belief in yourself, your product, or your idea, for that matter. Then all of a sudden, you don't believe in what you are doing, and you start to question yourself, asking if what you are doing even makes sense.

If you love what you are doing, then don't take it personally, and share less often with those people. You know who they are! Only share what you are doing with people who are on the same playing field with you, who believe in where you are going, and who are in harmony with you.

A rule I've learned is not to follow the majority of people. They generally do not know where they are going. They follow what everyone else is doing. You may have heard things like, *Get a good job with salary and benefits. That's security.* I've seen so many people who were laid off that thought they had "security" in a job. Listen, times are changing. Companies are downsizing; they are "doing more" with less.

When you are in business for yourself, you are in control of your paycheck and your time!

So, open your eyes and look for the opportunities and people that are going in their own direction. These are the people you want to pay attention to. These people are not following the crowd. They are people that know where they are going, and they are on a mission to get there. They have a purpose, and they are driven individuals.

Now, if you are in sales, one of the biggest frustrations I often hear is, *I don't have enough prospects and leads coming in, and customers are dropping off.*

My first question to you is, *What are you doing to bring prospects and leads in?* Sometimes I hear, *Well, I promote online, send out emails to email lists, build my list online, and so on.* Don't sit around waiting for people to come to you or call you. They don't. If you are waiting for this, you will be waiting a long time.

Sitting behind a computer is a slow and painful process if you are relying on this. I do believe these are good tools to have in place, but don't hide behind them.

Get out there and start selling your ideas, products, and services to people you don't know. Network. Talk to people. Create a habit of talking to everyone you meet about what you are doing. By doing this, you are going to get better and better at selling your idea.

Even if you have been in business for years, you need to keep selling. Sometimes in companies, an owner can get so busy working in their business that they stop selling their services or products, and sales start to drop. Never stop selling. Selling is what keeps you in business. It is what keeps your employees employed. Selling is what keeps adding profit to your bottom line. Your sales team needs to keep selling and always improving upon their sales techniques. Selling needs to be the top priority in every company and on every entrepreneur's mind.

Profit is the first order of business. Period!

If you've been in sales for years and are finding your sales decreasing, I would start to look at your sales cycle and what you are saying. Maybe you are bored with it and need to change it up. I am constantly changing up my approach because I want to get better and better.

Next… You've just sold your product or service, now what? Ask for the money! You're saying, of course, that's what you do; however, I've met so many people that are scared to ask for the money after they have sold something, scared to invoice the customer, or forget to invoice them. What???!!!

Don't let this be you! Get the money from them; invoice them, and remember to collect from them!

When you go to buy groceries, you don't say to the clerk, *I'll take these home. Then I'll send you the money.* No! You pay for the groceries before you leave the store. Collect the money. Then give them the product or service!

Do you sometimes feel as though you should give your service or product to them for free or give them a deal, especially if it's someone you know?

If you relate to this, ask yourself why you feel like you should give them a deal or give it to them for free. Then ask yourself if you are someone that always looks for a deal, a bargain, or even worse, looks for ways to get what you want for free. If this is you, that is your problem! Stop looking for things that are free. Stop looking for the cheapest deals; you get what you pay for. If it's a bargain, you get a bargain. If it's cheap, you are looking to get cheap back. Finding the best deal is not necessarily the best thing.

It's very simple; whatever you put out is what you can expect back. If you are constantly looking for the deals, the free stuff, then you can expect to have people come to you looking for deals, or they may ask you to give it to them for free. When you are constantly giving people deals just so you can make a sale, what you are really saying is you don't believe in what you are selling.

I had someone say to me once that I should cut him a deal. I also had someone tell me that I should give my time and service for free because I'm in the business of helping people. Let's just pretend I did that. If that's how I ran my business, how long do you think I would be in business? Not very long. I would be out of business very quickly. You are in business to provide a service or product and make a profit while doing it. It is very hard to live without it, so don't discount your products or services, and don't ask other people to discount their products or services either.

Besides, when people get things for free, many times they don't do anything with it. They don't take it seriously. They have no "skin in the game." It holds absolutely no value in that person's mind.

One of my mentors once told me that there are no shortcuts to success, and that advice always stuck with me. If you are someone who is always looking for a deal, or how you can get something for free, then guess what?

That is exactly what you are going to get. You are not working in harmony with the laws.

Free is not better. You get what you pay for.

If you are struggling with your sales, find someone who is doing what you want to be doing and follow them. Learn to be a good follower. If they are getting the results, they are doing something that is working. Ask if you can follow them, and when they tell you to do something, do it. Don't watch someone and then try to reinvent the wheel; that takes so much time!! Learn from them, implement what they are doing and, once things get going, then improve upon what you are doing. That is what they are doing. They are constantly improving upon what they are doing!

The second thing you need to do to raise your income level is increase the value or service you give and leave the impression of increase with people! This comes from the book *The Science of Getting Rich* by Wallace D. Wattles.

You need to provide more value to your customer than what you are taking from them in cash value. You need to leave everyone with the impression of increase, which means leaving them in a better place than when you first met. This is one of the principles to success!

This is so important, especially if you want repeat customers or clients. You want to develop lifers, people who stick with you because they believe in what you are doing, and they are reaping the benefits of coming in contact with you.

Lee Iacocca, American businessman, once said, *"Profit in business comes from repeat customers, customers that boast about your project or service and that bring friends with them."*

You have to make up your mind that you are going to be the best at what you do, that you want to be number one in your industry. How do you do this? You have to "perfect" what you are doing.

There are three things that the Law of Compensation states:

1. The need for what you do

2. Your ability to do it

3. The difficulty in replacing you

There most likely is a need for what you do. Most people don't spend any time working on number 2. They don't work on mastering what they are good at. You want to get really good at what you do, whether you are working in a company in a certain role or you are in business for yourself or you are an entrepreneur; you want to work every day to increase your ability to do what you are doing. Getting better every day, becoming better than you were yesterday, and giving your absolute best every day.

When you focus on working at improving your ability to do what you do, you will be difficult to replace. Your stock will go up.

These are simple things, and yet there is only a small percentage of people that actually implement these ideas. So how do you "perfect" what you do? Study! Again, I'm saying it. It is the only way. You need to be studying yourself because there is no one on earth that can do it for you. But you can do it for yourself, and the more you study you, the more you can become the best at what you do. Doing it better.

Here are two questions you should be asking yourself: *How can I provide more value? How can I make sure my customers or clients have the best experience by working with me? How can I become better at what I'm currently doing?*

These are questions I am constantly asking myself. This is the second order in my business. The first order of business is profit, and the second order is providing value.

Everyone on my team operates the same way. I don't budge on this. I am forever perfecting what I am doing and how I do it. Whether I am selling my service, doing a webinar for my clients, or speaking in front of large groups of people, I am constantly working on getting better at what I'm doing. The way I first started out in my business is not the way I'm doing it today. Why? Because I believe there is a better way to do absolutely everything. I believe that I can be better than I was yesterday. I believe my webinars can be better than they were the last time, I believe that my seminars and events can be better than they were the last time, I believe that my sales pitch can be better than it was the last time. The bottom line is, I am always looking at ways to improve my ability to do it.

Are you going to make mistakes? Yes. Are there going to be challenges? Yes. Learn from them. It's how you grow.

If you have a company, everyone on your team needs to understand this concept. If you are a one-man show, you need to understand this concept, even if you only have one client at the present moment.

If you don't have a client yet, it's simple; the first thing I would perfect is your sales pitch, your sales cycle, and getting your first client. You cannot provide a service to them until you sell something to them first. Once you have clients, then work on the next stage. You see, what can get in your way is trying to implement all of the processes all at once when you don't even have a customer or client yet. You will spend so much wasted energy and time doing that, and that is going to prolong you making money. You need to make money. Profit if first!

Get clients first. Then once you get your clients or customers, start working on perfecting your delivery methods. You will learn so much along the way, and you are going to be constantly changing up how you deliver.

Always think about how you can provide more value, more service, and increasing your sales! Always.

Chapter 6

Think and Act Like a Million Dollars

Think and act like a million dollars! Yes, you read right. You need to be thinking and acting like the person you want to become. This takes constant repetition and practice and should be included in your daily practices. If you don't have daily practices yet, then we need to talk about that too!

You may have heard of this concept before or heard something along the lines of "fake it until you make it."

But what does it really mean to do this?

I said something in the earlier chapters that I hope caught your attention, and I am going to repeat it again.

People earning $100,000 are not thinking and behaving the same as someone who is earning $50,000, and people who earn $500,000 do not think and act the same as someone earning $100,000, and so on. Someone earning $1,000,000 is thinking and behaving completely different from someone earning $500,000.

I want you to really think about this for a minute. Think of someone you know or know of who is earning what you want to be earning. There are things they are doing that are different from what you are currently doing.

Before you can change what you are doing, you first have to start thinking differently. You want to be thinking from the income level you want. So if you want to earn $200,000, then you want to ask yourself how that person would be thinking. What are some things they are doing differently? You can tell what a person is thinking by the results they are getting. Then compare it to what you are currently doing. How different is it? You will notice the difference.

Next, check your self-image. Most people think that self-image (or self-esteem or self-confidence) is the way people see you. That is part of it, but what is the image you have of yourself on the inside? How do you see yourself?

We have two parts to our self-image. The first is the outside image by the way you dress, talk, and behave, and the second part is the image that you hold of yourself on the inside. What do you believe to be true about yourself? How do you see yourself? What are you saying to yourself? What limiting beliefs do you have about yourself?

We operate from the inside out. Everything starts from within and then moves outward through our behavior and actions, and through your actions, you will create a result. It is the behavior that has to change for your results to change. You behavior controls your actions. And your paradigm controls your behavior. To change your behavior, you have to change your paradigm.

The problem is, when people want to make a change in their life, they are looking at the wrong things to change. They are looking at their conditions or circumstances or for other people to change first. They will say things like, *I can't change where I am, what I'm earning, where I live. Or I hear this often too, This is the hand I was dealt.*

The thing is, you can change it. You can change all of this no matter what your situation is, whether it's changing where you live, changing your job, increasing your income, or whatever it is that you want to change, you can, because it always starts with you.

You cannot change the outside – change conditions, change circumstances – until you change what's going on inside of you first. Simple.

When you want to begin this process, you first need to change your thinking and some of your beliefs when it comes to you. Whatever you believe to be true about yourself is what you are going to see and is ultimately going to show up in your results.

What can also happen is from the outside, we project a certain image, and yet what's going on in the inside is completely different from what you are projecting on the outside. This can cause a lot of doubt. Your confidence may be low; you might feel like a fraud and that you need to put on a façade.

There is a voice inside that could be saying, *Who am I to do this? I don't have the experience or the knowledge. They won't listen to me. I've never done this before.* Sound familiar? This is the inner dialogue and image I'm talking about.

If you believe that you are not good enough, this is what you will see, and it will affect your behavior. If you believe you are not smart enough or don't like the way you look, this is what you will see. You will only see all your imperfections and convince yourself of all kinds of excuses as to why you can't do what you want to do and talk yourself out of what you really want to do. How many times do you think you have done that to yourself? My guess is a lot. You are really good at talking yourself out of doing what you want to do and then justifying the reasons to yourself and other people.

All of these things I mentioned above, this is what everyone else will see because it will show through your behavior and actions. It will show up in the way you talk. It will show up in the way you present yourself. It will show up in your income. It will show up in how you earn a living. It will show up in how you perform as a professional. It will show up in every area of your life.

This is why it's so important to work with a mentor because they often see things in you that you can't see in yourself.

I want you to treat yourself well. I want you to start to see yourself as the person you want to become. This can be a hard thing for people to do. If you don't treat yourself well, with love and respect, then how can you expect others to? I don't mean in an egotistical or conceited way. Be good to yourself.

My mentor always tells me there is good in everything, no matter what the situation is. Look for the good. Now I've been through some tough situations too. We all have. We all have a story – things that have happened to us or things that we have done. Or maybe you have hurt someone. Everyone has been through something that has altered their natural state and caused them to think and feel a certain way.

Don't let these things define who you are. They are not who you are. They just happened to you, or you made a mistake, an error in judgment, or the ego got in the way. Holding onto them isn't going to help you. If you keep repeating the same negative story over and over to yourself and telling other people around you, you are repeating to yourself what you believe to be true. That becomes how you see yourself and how other people will see you.

Change it. Change your story.

"Everything that has happened to you is absolutely essential to who you are because it's giving you the tools to do what you need to do." Bob Proctor said this in a seminar one time, and it has stuck with me since then. There are things that we can hold onto for our whole life, causing us to look at it the wrong way.

When you change how you look at things, the things you look at will change. Maybe it's a lesson that we had to learn, to shake us up a bit, to point us in the right direction. Maybe something had to happen to allow something else to happen. When one door closes, another one will open. Don't let the past define you. It's not who you truly are.

Don't go around blaming other people, conditions, or circumstances for why you are where you are. The only person this ends up hurting is you.

You cannot change another person. You cannot change how another person thinks. You cannot change what another person does.

You can, however, change yourself. You can change the way you think and the way you look at things.

How do you move forward?

Create a new story for yourself. What do you want to see? How do you want to be seen? Who do you want to be known as? How do you want people to see you? How do you want your life to look? Who are the people in your life? These are things you want to think about. Ask yourself these questions, and write them down. Write out what you want to be like.

You are made with absolute perfection, and it is your job to bring that perfection to the surface.

I love what Steve Bow says, *"God's gift to us is more talent and ability than we'll ever hope to use in our lifetime. Our gift to God is to develop as much of that talent and ability as we can in this lifetime."*

How do you develop your talents and ability? Again, through study. How will you know what you are good at or how to perfect it unless you study yourself? When you start to study, you will gain an understanding of who you are and what you are capable of.

I teach people this every day. When people are working with me, I am teaching them how to study themselves. You are the most important person and resource, and you're the only way you can change your current circumstances. If your way is not working, then you need to try another way.

By now you may be asking, *What does your self-image have to do with profit and increasing your income?*

It has everything to do with it.

You can only go as far as your self-image will allow you to go. Do you have insecurities that get in the way? If you are in sales, some insecurities might be, *I'm too shy to go and talk to people. People are not going to listen to what I have to say. I don't have enough education. I am not successful. I don't feel comfortable talking to large groups. I don't like the way I speak. I don't like the way I look. I don't have a nice car to drive, and so on.* What is that voice inside saying to you? And believe it or not, if you have a team of people working for you, they too can have these insecurities that hold them back from performing.

You might also have some battle going on in your mind right now because a part of you might be thinking, *Well, I have a good self-image. I live in a nice house. I drive a nice car. I dress nice, I have lots of friends. I believe I can double or triple my income,* etc.

I know for sure that if you are reading this book right now, then you want to be doing better than you are currently doing. Well, then you need to check in with your self-image because your self-image is set to what you are currently doing and earning.

The first step is to be honest with yourself. Stop pretending. If you are not getting the desired results that you want, and you are not currently where you want to be right now, then you have some work to do. Otherwise, you would be where you want to be.

You want to make sure your thoughts, feelings, and actions are aligned. You can be saying one thing and doing something contradictory to what you are thinking and saying.

When I work with people, I don't go by what they say because generally people say a lot. They want you to believe something about themselves. They want you to believe that they are smart, successful, and have everything together. I have been trained to go by what their actual results show. I listen to what they are saying, and then I look at the results. Most of the time, they are not aligned.

Don't take this as a negative because I study this, and I know that all of this can change for them or you. You want to learn to always go by results as well.

Where you are is only an indication of what you are currently thinking and feeling. It's not where you are headed if you decide to change.

If you want to know what your self-image is and what you believe to be true, then take a look at your results. Positive or negative, that is what you believe to be true.

All successful people are constantly working on their self-image whether they realize it or not. I am aware of what self-image is, and it is something I am constantly working on. The more I work on myself, the better a person I become, the more money I make. Simple.

Study successful people. They are constantly working on getting better at what they are doing so they can earn more and do more. They're perfecting their craft. They understand who they are. They have developed certain habits, they are very disciplined, and they are very focused and productive individuals. They surround themselves with people of the same mindset. They have developed a sense of urgency. They get a lot done in a short amount of time.

Most people think that earning more money requires more work. This is just a belief. Most people were taught that you have to work harder to earn more. Hard work, I believe, comes from developing certain habits and disciplines within yourself and developing a mental toughness to keep going. Developing persistence. It doesn't mean physically working harder. You are going to burn out if you are physically working harder, and worse yet, you are going jeopardize your health in doing so.

It's not about working harder. It's about working smarter. There is a better way to do everything you are doing now. The best way hasn't been thought of yet. The best way to do something hasn't been done yet. You can be doing so much better than what you are currently doing. Everyone can. You are not operating at your full capacity.

Earning more money doesn't have to require more work for you. The more you work on you and understand who you are, the more you will increase your confidence. You will begin to see how to become more effective, increase your productivity and performance, and improve the way you do things, which will all lead to increasing your income.

If I am burning out, then I know I am not working smart, and I need to change what I am doing. Sometimes it is in the simplest things. Changing even the smallest things in your performance can make the biggest difference.

For example, how do you spend your time? Are there things that you are currently doing that waste a lot of time and energy. For example, how much TV do you watch? How much time do you spend scrolling through social media? How much time do you use procrastinating on starting or finishing projects?

Are you giving your absolute best every day? If you are frustrated, it's time to change all of this. To improve, ask yourself how you want to see yourself.

You can create a new self-image. This takes study, practice, and repetition. It doesn't happen overnight, but if you stay with it, it will happen.

Find someone who is doing what you want to do. Follow them. I've said this before. Study them. Study what they are doing. Study their habits. Study their behaviors.

I do this. I have someone I'm following. I watch them very closely. I learn from them. I pay attention to detail. I pay attention to the way they speak, the way they explain things, and I often find myself saying things they say. If I like something particular in someone that I think can help me, I will adapt to that new behavior. My self-image has changed so much in the past few years, but I'm constantly working on it. I am still the same person, but I am becoming better and better at what I'm doing. I am working at bringing out my strengths. That's what you want to do.

You have so many strengths. What are they? If I asked you what your weaknesses are, you would have a whole list ready right away because we were programmed to focus on what's wrong, what's wrong with this situation, and what's wrong with us. Instead, focus on what you are good at. What do you like about yourself? In the beginning, this may take time to see and feel awkward, but keep asking yourself what you like about yourself.

Once you have your new self-image written out, begin to act "as if." Act as if you are that person. This may create discomfort, and there is part of you that is going to say things like, *I'm not this person. That's not who I truly am. Who do I think I am?* The people around you will start to see the changes, and they may not like or agree because they still see you as the old you.

Realize they are not you. You have a responsibility to look after yourself, and what you want to do it is ultimately up to you.

I love what Wallace D Wattles said: "*To become the best, surround yourself by the best.*"

You deserve the best! Don't doubt it. Just decide that you do!

Chapter 7

Time to Manifest What You Want!

Depending on where your awareness level is right now, you may have heard or read some of what I have written about in this book. But I'm going to be frank with you.

Knowing is not enough! I said this in the earlier chapters.

You can know all kinds of stuff. You can know exactly what to do. You can be a really good student too. You can be great at gathering all kinds of information. You can be the ultimate student, studying all the books of our time from our great leaders, successful business people, self-help books, get rich books, manifesting books and prosperity books.

It is really simple, though. Nothing is going to happen until you change your thinking and begin to take some action.

Action. This is what you need. You need to move into action. It does not matter how much you know. Remember when I was talking about awareness and about how there are some people who have degrees at the end of their names to show that they know a lot, yet their results show that they are broke. On the other side, there are people who have very little knowledge, and they are making it happen; they are very wealthy.

We do not operate from the basis of how much we know. We don't. Knowledge is essential, but it is the understanding of how to apply the knowledge we have that is crucial. And what gets in our way of applying what we know is our paradigm. Our beliefs, our habits, and our behaviors; it's how we are programmed. If we are not programmed to do what we know how to do, it doesn't matter how much knowledge we have because we won't do it.

There is a huge issue going on where we have students accumulating massive debt because they were taught that to be successful you have to go to school. Then they graduate from school and can't find a job. This may occur because they don't have the experience or because they are expecting more in the opportunity department, simply because of their education. Knowledge is key, but it's never about how much you know. It's how much you do with that knowledge.

If you are young and are reading my book, go out there and get some experience. Leave your pride at the door, and start at the bottom and work your way up. You will learn so much by doing this. You will create great habits, discipline, work ethics and so on, and that experience is invaluable.

The older you get, the more you know, but the less you do. Why is this? Because you have created certain habits and patterns in your way of living and are set in your ways. You believe certain things, and you have not changed what you are doing or what you believe. You may feel that your way is the right way because this was the way you were taught and the way you have always been doing it. The truth is, the way to do things is always changing regardless if you decide to change or not.

There is another huge problem I see every day. Baby Boomers are forced into early retirement. They are let go and given the golden handshake. They've been with the company for forty plus years. It's all they know. It's all they've done. They are taken out of their environment that has been their experience and knowledge to-date and put into the unknown world in which we live in today.

Things are so different from when they first started out in their careers. The way to do things has changed so much. The way to communicate has evolved and transformed. The way to get clients has changed. Their world is completely different than it used to be.

As a result of their company's needs changing, they are doing more with less. And what is happening is occurring because the company is changing its way, but the people in the company are not changing. Their beliefs never altered, and they were forced into a world that is unfamiliar to them. We were never taught to keep reevaluating what we believe to be true. Take a look at what you believe right now. To find out what you believe, look at your results. Your results will tell you what you believe to be true. When you analyze your beliefs, if they are not serving you anymore, you can form new beliefs, beliefs that are in harmony with where you want to go.

Our world is not getting bigger; it's getting smaller. You can text, call, send pictures, send videos and connect with people all over the world with the push of a button.

The way we do things now is not the way we did them five years ago, ten years ago, or twenty years ago. It's changing, and it's changing every day. Just look at how much phones have changed in the past twenty years. Our phones are like mini computers now.

Do you see how important it is to study this? How important it is to study yourself? If you don't study yourself and keep changing the way you look at things or changing the way you do things, you are going to get left behind because the world is not stopping. We are making some of the greatest advancements of our time, and people are rising up. It can be very exciting to some and yet very scary to others.

Look at the changes just in the past ten years. Look at how the internet has changed, how we communicate with people around the world. Imagine another ten years from now and what it will look like.

There are people and companies that are constantly improving upon what they are doing. Improving the service they provide, improving the functionality of products, making it better than it was last year.

This also applies to you. You have to change what you are doing. Take a look at what you are currently doing. How can you make it better? Is it working? Change occurs whether you agree with it or like it. You have a choice – you can stay the same, or you can improve just like everything else is improving around us. The best way to do something hasn't been thought of yet. There is always a better way to do everything. I suggest you develop the same belief! It's a good belief to change. Your way is not necessarily the best way.

If you are doing something and are not getting the results you want, then stop doing it. Try another way. Try another approach. It sounds simple, but this is so easily missed because you might not even be aware of what you are currently doing, so a new way might not stand out to you. That's why it's important that you study and that you check in with yourself regularly on where you are at with your goal. Are you on track? Are you seeing results? Are you seeing improvements?

Your goal doesn't change, but the plan can change. You are going to be course correcting the whole way, trying to figure it out.

If this were easy, everyone would be doing it. Everyone would be earning what he or she wants to be earning. Everyone would be where he or she wants to be right now.

Don't fall for the get rich schemes out there. Everyone is trying to make a dollar. There is so much noise out there with all kinds of people telling you how to make money, how to make millions – invest in this, invest in that. You may have implemented some of these ideas and have not been successful.

Some of them are probably very good, but are you following the formula exactly? What happens is you will invest in something to help yourself, but you don't do the work required to get there, or you don't follow the process exactly. You start it, but don't finish it. Get to the bottom of this once and for all because you are going to keep wasting your time and money if you don't get to the root of the problem. There is no other way. You want to find out why you are currently doing what you are doing and then change what you are doing if it's not working.

Sound simple? Think again. Think of how many times you tried to change something, and you've always gone back to your old ways.

I love this quote from Robin Sharma, *"Change is hard in the beginning, messy in the middle and beautiful in the end."*

Changing the way you've always done things is not easy, but it gets easier when you know how to do it the right way. And you need a system and process in place to help with this. Change is hard in the beginning. It's hard because you are going against everything you are currently doing, currently believe to be true, so it's going to seem foreign to you and make you feel uncomfortable.

Remember the word I lightly introduced earlier. Paradigm? Your paradigm is constantly going off, giving you every reason, every excuse, every justification, every belief of why staying where you are is better for you. Even if it means you have to settle, your paradigm is telling you why it's a good idea, convincing you why you should stay where you are.

It doesn't want you to change. It's more comfortable there.

Before you can have more, you have to first become more. You have to get to the root cause, and change it there first, and what you want to change is your paradigm.

Your paradigm is a multitude of habits and behaviors stored in a section of your subconscious mind.

There are things you are currently doing, and you know you shouldn't be doing them, but you still are.

You are procrastinating on things. If you are in sales, you know you should be making those calls, getting out there. You have all of the tools you need to be successful. The only thing that is holding you back is you.

Where do you start? You want to change your programming, which I mentioned in earlier chapters.

Think of it like this; I have an iPhone, and it seems like every month, I am getting notices that I need to install the latest version of the software. The latest software is upgrading my phone's programming. It's upgrading how my phone operates, how my phone functions, the speed of my phone, and it's getting rid of the bugs and installing new tools and applications, so the phone functions better.

This is what you need to do with yourself. What you need to do with your mind. Your mind is the most powerful resource you have. Everything starts out in your mind. You want to upgrade the programming in your mind, clean out all of the viruses. Improve functions, which is improving how you operate, enhancing your thinking and installing a new habit or belief.

If your beliefs are not serving you, get rid of them.

You can try doing this on your own. Most people attempt to do it on their own because it will cost them less money. But honestly, how much cheaper is it really? Your time is worth something. How long do you want to keep "trying" to figure it out?

How's that working for you? I used to do that. I wanted to see if I could do it on my own first. Ask yourself how much time and energy you have wasted doing that.

Did you follow the formula? Most don't follow the formula. Most people will agree with what they are reading, but they will either apply none of what they have learned, or bits and pieces of what they read, or they will start out and do well in the beginning but quit. Why? Because it's hard. Because it feels unnatural to them. They feel unbalanced and out of sorts.

When you quit, what you are saying to yourself is you would rather settle for what you have than go after what you want.

Here's an example. You have probably been on a diet at some point in your life, and you make the decision that this is the time you are going to do it. So you start changing your eating habits, your activity level, and spend more time exercising.

You start out well. You get off to a great start. Your weight starts to go down, and your muscles start to tighten. More importantly, you begin to feel really good.

Then one night, you say to yourself, *Gosh, I've done amazing. I feel really good. You know what? I deserve a few chips. I've done so well that I deserve a little treat for all of my efforts.*

What just happened there? Your paradigm just convinced you that it was okay to eat those chips. Then you might say to yourself, *OMG, this is good. You know what? I don't want to be the person who is constantly watching what I eat or my weight. I love food. That's no way to live…* and so on.

Sound familiar? It's over. You are now back to your old way of thinking and your old habits. And soon you've gained all of the weight back. The change that occurred, in the beginning, was only temporary. Unless you make changes at the root of the problem, you will only experience temporary changes, so this is why your results may always go up and down.

How about this example? You have decided that this is the year you are getting out of debt. You are paying those cards off; you are watching what you spend. You do well in the beginning, and you start to see the balance go down, and it makes you start to feel happy. You're making progress.

Then one day, your paradigm tells you, *Sara, look at what you have done. Your debt is almost paid off. You're doing amazing. Look at how hard you have worked to do this. Look at how much you have sacrificed to do this.*

Sara is thinking, *Yeah, you're right. Look at how well I'm doing. I've paid off almost all my cards. I've worked hard to do this. I deserve something for this! Just something small, that's it. It's my reward for doing so well.* So, Sara goes out and buys herself something that she loves. She didn't have the money for it because all she has done is paid down her cards.

It's over. You've just gone back to your old way of thinking, and in no time, those cards are maxed out again. One excuse will lead to another, which will lead to a multitude of excuses, and you've convinced yourself it was okay to do this. You've justified every reason to yourself. Then, when you've maxed your cards out again, you are still justifying why you did it. This happens all of the time.

Sara hasn't done anything to increase her income, to increase her profit. She has just scrimped and saved and cut things out. There is a desire in you to want more, and that's natural. It's a good thing to want more because the "wanting" part is a creative stage. We should live like that and live the way we want to live.

But if you are not breaking this habit and increasing your income to match what you want, you are going to get into financial difficulties. Even if you pay off all of your debt, you will most likely end up back in debt because you are going to want more of something later on, and you still won't have the money for it. This is a habit and behavior. If you want more, just make sure you are increasing your income. Then, start to look for ways you can do that.

You might think about it from moment to moment, but are you doing anything about it? As soon as you embark on something new that you haven't experienced before, fear kicks in, discomfort sets in, and you start to feel uneasy with what you are doing. At that moment, you decide that maybe what you have is not so bad, and you settle.

I was given important advice early on in my journey. They said to me "*Jacquelyn, never settle.*"

I think about that often because there are so many times we are settling; you are settling. Settling for what you have.

Settling doesn't just mean material-type stuff. That's not what I'm talking about. I'm talking about you, where you are, what you are doing, what you currently have in your life.

I am working on increasing profit in my business every day. Earning a profit is very important to me, but it's not about the money for me. It never is and never will be. It never is for most people. It's what the money can do. It allows you to extend the service that you provide. My "profit" goes right back into my business so I can do more and use it to create more. To provide more service. The service I provide today is not the same as I provided when I first started out because as I get better at what I'm doing, the service I provide is getting better.

Don't get me wrong. I like nice things. I too have learned to treat myself well. But that is not my reason for earning more money. It helps me live the life-style I want, it pays for my standard of living, and it makes me comfortable.

Everyone's standard of living is different. You create your standard of living the way you want to, not by how you should or how other people think you should.

I believe in three things we are meant to do:

1. Create the life we want
2. Live the way we want to live and
3. Be happy

Whatever those three things mean to you is all that matters. Here is the cool thing; you can keep creating a new standard of living. It doesn't have to stay the same. You are in control of that.

We are here to grow, learn, and experience.

The way to grow is by continuing to invest in you, study you, study who you are, what you are doing, how you are doing, and then improving and mastering your craft.

Everything I am telling you in this book I have done and I'm still doing. I would not be writing this and telling you to do something if I had not done it myself.

There are a lot of people out there who do that. They write on prosperity and how to increase your income, but they have yet to apply it to their lives.

I've done everything I am telling you. I have changed habits, changed what I'm doing, changed the way I am thinking, changed my self-image, put myself out there. I've changed the way I talk and speak to people, sales, I mean everything. I've had naysayers, and I've been turned down a lot, but I've developed something inside myself to keep going, to show up every day, no matter what, and keep improving what I am doing.

Everything that I've done has helped me earn thousands of dollars, and all I did was study and work on me. You know what? I'm just getting started. I have a monster goal, but I also have a lot I want to do and many people I want to help along the way. You see, it's never about the money; it's what the money can do. It allows you to extend yourself far beyond your own physical presence.

I have clients that I have been working with for only four months, and a few days ago, they texted me and said, "*Jacquelyn, we did it. We reached our goal of $90,000 in one month!*" They have a small business, eight to ten people, and here is the amazing thing – their business is not even a year old. They are very smart, and they got involved in studying this information. Then they introduced it to their whole team. As a result of that, they see their bottom line improve!

This doesn't happen by chance or luck; it happens by design. They created it, just like I created my results, and you can create your results. It is such an amazing feeling when you take charge!

Create Permanent Results That Last

There are only two ways to change habits or behaviors:

1. Constant spaced repetition
2. Through an emotional impact

Emotional impacts are typically a negative response to a situation, so that leaves repetition as the best way.

You cannot change habits in one day or read something once and expect changes to occur. This takes constant practice and repetition of planting new ideas into your subconscious mind. It is the only way to change habits, and this takes daily practice and discipline.

I've mentioned this several times throughout my book, and I'm going to mention it again because it is so important, and yet most people don't want to do it. They say they want to improve their finances, but they don't do the work or make the required changes to get them where they want to go.

You will need a study routine. You will need to know how to study yourself. You should have a mentor or a system and tools that you can use. You need to follow someone who knows how to do this. I've given you some tips in this book, and you can start with those.

You also need to work on your mindset and prepare it. You will want to prepare your mind for success. Prepare your mind for what you want to achieve.

Think of athletes and the amount of time and money they spend on training, training themselves how to do better, to become the best at what they do.

The number of hours they spend on visualizing the outcome, visualizing how they want the game to go. They prepare their mind before a game or an event. They are prepared. This is exactly what you need to do to multiply your income.

Athletes don't just wake up one day and say, I'm going to win the gold medal at the Olympics, and off they go. They train. They prepare. They work. They correct. They do what it takes. They get hurt along the way and have sore muscles, but they keep going because they build up their endurance; they develop a mental toughness to get them through the harder times. They know when they get to the finish line, it will have been worth it.

This is what it takes. Here is where the work begins. The hard work. Remember, I said that hard work is developing the mental toughness, the discipline, the habits and the persistence. This is how it begins. It's doing small things in a certain way.

Every action you take today will bring you closer to where you want to be. As soon as you take a step, the next step will present itself, but you won't see it until you take the step.

This is hard for some people to do because they want to know the "how." How is this going to happen? As soon as they start thinking about the how and look at their current evidence, they give up. They think nothing is happening; it's not working. The things they require are not there. This can play mind games with someone who doesn't understand what is happening.

Let's go back to the athlete. His coach is telling him to make minor improvements to his stride or the way he holds his hands. To the athlete, it feels weird. It feels uncomfortable because he is not used to it, but he continues to do it. At first, it seems like he has gotten worse and is actually going backward, but his coach is telling him to keep going, keep practicing every day until it becomes natural, even though at that moment, he doesn't see it and is questioning this. After constant repetition of doing the same thing over and over again, it takes root, it becomes natural, and they are off. Just making those minor adjustments increased their performance.

When you set your goal, you are not going to see how this will unfold. Think about this. Think about something you were going after that you achieved. At the time, you didn't know how you were going to get there. You just wanted it so bad that you did what it took to get it.

It works the same way when you want to increase your income and increase the profit. It just seems different to you because this has to do with money and increasing your income. Your paradigm might be telling you no, it's different. It's not different. It's the same formula.

It comes down to a mind game. You must understand the mind. Most successful people are what you would call "unconscious competents." Even they don't know exactly what they are doing. They just keep doing it.

Imagine becoming a conscious competent, understanding what is happening when it's happening. Understanding how to create the results you want. Knowing that you will receive everything you always require on time.

Here's the thing: as you keep taking action and keep focusing on your goal, you will attract everything you need to help you fulfill your goal. Everything!

Resources, people, and opportunities will show up. Successful people love people who take action. Who get results. Who help themselves. Who aren't scared to put themselves out there. Who have some skin in the game. Who are prepared to risk everything.

Do you know why they love these kinds of people? Because they have been there! They have been down this road. They know what it takes.

What I am writing about isn't for lightweights, even if you think you've heard it before or know it.

I've worked really hard. I've developed a mental toughness. I've done things that most people aren't even aware of, even people closest to me. Success is very quiet, but it always leaves a trail.

I don't like to talk about what I'm doing until I've done it. I don't like to give advice until I've done it. I'm not going to tell someone what to do until I've gotten results myself. I didn't want to write this book until I had the results to show for it.

When you begin to study you, you gain an understanding of who you are as a person. You learn what your strengths are, and you improve upon what you are doing.

"Understanding is really the key to freedom." My mentor says this all the time, but it took me a bit to figure out what he meant by this.

When you start to understand, you move forward with faith based on understanding. Knowing that you will receive everything you require at the exact moment in time when you need it, not when you "think" you need it, but when you actually need it. There is a huge difference between the two.

Your job now is to recognize the opportunities and the signs when they are in front of you, and go for it. Sometimes it's as large as a billboard, sometimes it's a conversation, and sometimes it's being in the right place at the right time.

You need to take daily action steps. Get out of your comfort level, and get uncomfortable. Make sure your action steps are aligned with your goal, and you don't want to keep busy for the sake of keeping busy.

When you begin to feel uncomfortable, it is a sign that you are growing, that you are moving in the right direction. Why? Because you have never been on this path before. You've never experienced this, so it makes you feel uncomfortable.

The uncomfortableness is a sign you are stretching and growing. If you want to do something you've never done before, then you have to be willing to experience what you've never experienced before.

When you change habits, it is going to make you uncomfortable. Changing your routine is going to make you uncomfortable. When you begin to act like the person you want to become, it's going to be uncomfortable. Get tough with yourself.

I have a saying that I use with my clients, *"Get comfortable being uncomfortable."* If you feel uncomfortable, you are on the right track!

Create daily habits that work for you. Work on one or two at a time. When you work on too many at once, you are going to become frustrated. How do you know you've changed a habit? When your result changes. If they haven't changed, then keep working on it.

There are things I'm working on every day because I haven't changed them yet.

A lot of people suffer from procrastination, indecision, poor time management skills and a lack of motivation.

The first thing is, you can't manage time. We all get the same amount of hours in a day. I get no more hours than you do. What you can manage is the activities and where you spend your time during the day. The first place to start is taking a look at how you are spending your time. What are you doing? Do you plan out your day beforehand, are you productive, do you get a lot done?

Multitasking! It's not a great thing. This word, multitasking, has made its way into our daily lives, convincing us that we are getting a lot done! The truth is, it creates more disorder than anything else. We are not able to focus on more than one thing at a time. We can't. You are only able to give your attention and energy to one thing. So instead of multitasking, try focusing on one project, and see it through to the end. Then move onto the next project. Multitasking creates so many projects, and you become overwhelmed because you have a lot of things started but nothing finished.

Next, every night before you go to bed or before you leave the office, write out six goal-achieving activities that you want to complete the next day. Do this every day so you don't have to think about what you want to accomplish when you wake up. It's already done, and you can be on your way. Make sure these activities are aligned with your goal.

Procrastination – well, this you need to work on. Procrastination can come from being indecisive, not making a decision about what you are going to do, so you procrastinate. Sometimes there is fear attached to what you want to do, so you inadvertently procrastinate.

How about discipline? Discipline is when you give yourself a command and follow it. How many times do you say you are going to do something, but you don't follow through with it? Work on following through with commitments you make, decisions you make, and so on. You want to be able to lead yourself in the direction you want to go.

Imagine what would change if you worked on just a few of these habits. A lot would probably change. And where would it lead? Right to the bottom line.

How do you overcome procrastination, become more disciplined, and create order in your day? You got it – through studying you!

My advice is, if you are not where you want to be right now on your own, get some skin in the game, and invest in you. Get yourself a mentor. Spend some time and money on studying you, and find a system to help you create what you want. Don't rely on freebies. Free information is not going to get you anywhere. Free information; that's exactly what it is. It's free, and free holds absolutely no value. I'm saying this because I used to do this. I used to "try" to do it by myself, learn by myself, scour the internet for information, free webinars, free videos, self-help books, etc.

Get yourself a mentor, someone who knows how to do this work, and follow the instructions. You can try to do it on your own, but chances are if you are not where you want to be right now, then doing it on your own is not working. I suggest you find someone who knows this and understands how it all works.

Mentors see things in you that you can't see in yourself because you are focused on what you see with your eyes. Your mentor will see what is within you.

Repetition is key. We learn through repetition. If you've only read this book once, read it again. Read it several times. I guarantee what's in this book isn't going to change, but what will change is you will see something inside yourself that you didn't see before.

If you want to make massive changes and increase the profit in your life, then you'd better get serious. You are not getting any younger. The change always starts right now, right where you are with what you have.

Don't be the person who keeps saying, *I'll wait until I have more time, more money, when I'm in a better place, or in a better circumstance.* How long have you been saying that? Don't let any more time go by!

Increasing your income and increasing your profit always starts with you first. You must gain an understanding of yourself and of money and profit and how to bring it into your life and keep it in your life. You don't want short-term success; you want to create long-term success.

Profit is the first order of business. Period. It allows you to enjoy your life the way you were designed to enjoy it.

I am forever grateful that I spent the time and money learning this, studying me, because this is exactly what has put me in the 1% of income earners. This is just the beginning for you. Get excited about where you are going. Know that you can do this. You can have what you want. I know that you can do it because I have done it. I am no different than you. I just learned how to apply what's in this book and how to do things in a certain way.

Get serious about you! Adding more profit in your life will increase the quality of your life in so many ways. It will allow you to do the things you truly want to do and allow you to live the way you want to live. Do whatever you have to do to raise your income so you can enjoy life as you want to. You will look back and be so grateful you did.

We are here for a short period, so make the most of it! Find out what makes you happy! Profit doesn't just have to apply to money all the time. You can add profit to every area of life. We live in an abundant world full of opportunity. Grab a hold and enjoy the ride! I'm here to tell you that you can do all of this by making a decision today with where you are and with what you have right now. That's what I did. I am forever grateful for taking the time when I did to study these principles and learn how to apply them, and because I was able to do it, so can you!

Afterword

Almost 39 years ago, when I was at the young age of 19, I went to a Bob Proctor seminar that totally changed my life forever. I heard Bob Proctor say the following: "No amount of reading or memorizing will make you successful in life. It is the understanding and application of wise thought that counts."

If you think about that quote for a moment, there is wisdom in those words. And, if you look closely, you will discover Bob is also making a recommendation. Bob suggests seeking a level of understanding so that you can and will apply these *wise thoughts*.

Jacquelyn MacKenzie, like me, is an avid student. She studies and teaches these materials and she has a deep level of understanding. She has created a priceless resource that has the potential to change your life in only positive ways. I am grateful for her writing this book. It is rare to discover anyone who has the depth of understanding that Jacquelyn has and she has taken that understanding and created this gift for you in the form of a book.

Now that you have finished this book, here's what I recommend that you do. Go back to the beginning and carefully review all the chapters. Get a study partner and together review the chapters from this book and share your insights. Do this daily. Another familiar quote I am reminded of is: "If you read a book the second time, you don't see something in it you didn't see before, you see something in yourself that wasn't there before."

Are you ready to grow? Are you ready to be truly rich, in every way? Now is the time. You are holding the answer in your hands.

I believe this book, *The Prophet of Profit*, is destined to become a classic. I see this book on everyone's book-shelf. In my imagination, I am observing people sharing how THIS book made a difference in their life. You may not ever require another self-help book.

Jacquelyn MacKenzie knows what she is talking about. One of my favorite lines in this book is the following where she said: "Everything you need to get to your goal is already here." I believe Jacquelyn meant that the potential is available to you, and I believe the answer to how to achieve your goals can be found on the pages of this book.

Peggy McColl
New York Times Best Selling Author

About the Author

 Jacquelyn began her business career in 1999 working in the commercial construction management industry. Very quickly her career took off like a rocket! Despite starting in business at twenty, she knew what it took to get results!

After raising her 3 young boys, Jacquelyn joined the Proctor Gallagher Institute in 2014 to work alongside Bob Proctor teaching the *Thinking Into Results* leadership program. Thinking Into Results is the most powerful business transformational program of its kind.

Jacquelyn has become a leading Consultant in the world within the Proctor Gallagher Institute. Working with Jacquelyn creates phenomenal results! She brings the impact of Bob Proctor's proven formula into both large and small businesses and she is dedicated to teaching organizations and individuals how to unleash the full potential.

To learn more about Jacquelyn MacKenzie please visit her Website:
www.jacquelynmackenzie.com

To take advantage of a free 1:1 coaching session, send an email to:
info@jacquelynmackenzie.com

Made in the USA
Middletown, DE
15 May 2017